LAUNCH

Biblical Help for Moving Your Teen or Young Adult into the Real World

Chap Bettis

Unless otherwise indicated, all Scripture quotations are from the ESV® Bible (The Holy Bible English Standard Version®), copyright © 2001 by Crossway, a publishing ministry of Good News Publishers. Used by permission. All rights reserved.

Scripture quotations marked (NIV) are taken from the Holy Bible, New International Version®, NIV®. Copyright © 1973, 1978, 1984 by Biblica, Inc.™ Used by permission of Zondervan. All rights reserved worldwide. www.zondervan.com. The "NIV" and "New International Version" are trademarks registered in the United States Patent and Trademark Office by Biblica, Inc.™

Scripture quotations marked CSB have been taken from the Christian Standard Bible®, Copyright © 2017 by Holman Bible Publishers. Used by permission. Christian Standard Bible® and CSB® are federally registered trademarks of Holman Bible Publishers.

Launch: Biblical Help for Moving Your Teen or Young Adult into the Real World
Copyright © 2024 Chap Bettis.
Diamond Hill Publishing
All rights reserved.
ISBN: 978-0-9990410-6-2

Without limiting the rights under copyright reserved above, no part of this publication may be reproduced, stored in, or introduced into a retrieval system, or transmitted, in any form, or by any means (electronic, mechanical, photocopying, recording, or otherwise) without the prior written permission of the copyright owner.

The scanning, uploading, and distribution of this book via the internet or via any other means without the permission of the publisher is illegal and punishable by law. Please purchase only authorized electronic editions and do not participate in or encourage electronic piracy of copyrighted materials. Your support of the author's rights is appreciated.

While the author has made every effort to provide accurate internet addresses at the time of publication, neither the publisher nor the author assumes any responsibility for errors or for changes that occur after the publication. Further, the publisher does not have any control over and does not assume any responsibility for third-party websites or their content.

For more information or for a free audiobook of
The Disciple-Making Parent, visit www.thedisciplemakingparent.com.

OTHER BOOKS FROM CHAP BETTIS

The Disciple-Making Parent: A Comprehensive Guidebook for Raising Your Children to Love and Follow Jesus Christ

Managing Your Households Well: How Family Leadership Trains You for Church Leadership

Parenting with Confidence: Biblical Truth in a Chaotic World (Video Workbook)

Parenting with Patience: Overcoming Anger in the Home (Video Workbook)

The Disciple-Making Parent's Donut Date Journal: 70 Questions to Connect You to Your Child's Heart

The Disciple-Making Parent's Donut Date Journal Family History Edition: 70 Questions for Children to Ask Their Parents

CONTENTS

THEOLOGICAL FOUNDATIONS

1 LAUNCH TIME! · 9

2 TOWARD A THEOLOGY OF AGE · 17

3 LAUNCH OBJECTIVES · 25

PRACTICAL APPLICATIONS

4 LAUNCHING TO A RESIDENTIAL COLLEGE · 35

5 LAUNCHING WHILE STAYING AT HOME · 43

6 STILL AT HOME WHEN THEY SHOULDN'T BE · · · · · · · · · · · · · · · · · · · 51

7 FINAL THOUGHTS · 61

THEOLOGICAL FOUNDATIONS

1
LAUNCH TIME!

Like arrows in the hands of a warrior are the children of one's youth.
Blessed is the man who fills his quiver with them!
He shall not be put to shame
when he speaks with his enemies at the gate. (Ps. 127:4-5)

"How do I disciple my eighteen-year-old?" "Do you have any advice for me as my children approach the adult years and leave home?" "How should I be thinking about sending my child to college?"

I hear these and similar questions at every conference that I speak at. And I understand that pain. As a young father I wanted to be intentional in my parenting. When my children were young, I read a number of resources that helped give me a strong foundation.[1] Later, I also began to understand biblical principles of discipleship appropriate to the ages of my children. That material is found in my book *The Disciple-Making Parent* and forms the basis of our ministry.[2]

But when my children hit the late teen years and early college years, I found myself floundering. I discovered numerous resources to help Christian students as they went off to college. But I could not find anything to help the parent. I found myself unsure through that period. As a result, I determined to try and think biblically about principles that should guide us through that time of a child's life. That's what you have in your hands today.

As disciple-making parents, our goal is for our children to grow up to love and follow Jesus Christ. We want them to be not just disciples but disciple-makers. We pray they will be young men and young women who stand like Daniel and Esther in our chaotic culture and who seek to take the gospel to the nations. The years of eighteen to twenty-two are crucial in setting the trajectory of a person's life. Though we cannot nor should not control our children, we can aim them in the right direction. We can seek to "launch" them well.

The goal of this modest booklet is to help you do just that: launch your high schooler into the young adult years. It is the booklet I wish I had when my children were at that stage. My prayer is that it will help you have a positive vision for that launch and avoid the problems that can occur during this time.

Arrows or Aircraft?
When Sharon and I were in the midst of raising our four children, we often heard speakers use the metaphor of an arrow from Psalm 127.

> Like arrows in the hands of a warrior are the children of one's youth. Blessed is the man who fills his quiver with them! He shall not be put to shame when he speaks with his enemies at the gate. (Psalm 127:4-5)

Children, we were told, are like arrows to be developed and then shot out. We found this scripture helpful to remind us of a number of biblical truths: We are raising children in the midst of a spiritual battle. Discipling children who love Jesus Christ and his church is one way we participate in that battle. We, as parents, have the incredible privilege of shaping these young lives. In addition, this metaphor reminded us that arrows are not meant to stay in the quiver. They are meant to fly out to accomplish their purpose.

There is only one, very big problem with the application these speakers were making. Children are not inanimate arrows! They have a mind of their own. You can aim and shoot a child in one direction, and they can decide to go the exact opposite way.

Launching an Aircraft
Instead, it might also be helpful to think of the transition to adulthood like that of launching an airplane from an aircraft carrier. Why do I like this analogy as well?

First, like the arrow, it reminds us that our ultimate goal is to send our children out into the world to make their mark. They are not meant to stay at home forever. Rather we want to raise them to stand strong as salt and light in our broken world, taking the gospel to the nations.

Second, launching from an aircraft carrier reminds us we are not in ultimate control. Another individual commands the plane. While the arrow is passive, the pilot of an aircraft is not. After the launch, he is the one who controls the airplane. The ship can now only communicate with the pilot.

Finally, not all launches go as planned. Perhaps you have seen film from the early days of aircraft carriers during World War II. Airplanes, fully loaded with fuel and weapons, took off from the ship's deck. Sometimes, after the plane launched, it dipped precariously below the deck as it gained speed to fly. At other times there were launch malfunctions leading to a plane ditching in the sea.

Thankfully, launch problems are not common in our modern military. However, they are common in our families. Sometimes, after we launch our child, we see them fly at half throttle below the level that we launched them. At other times, they can be like pilots who ignore their training and head in a completely different direction. And unfortunately, there can be those that do not launch successfully and end up ditching in the sea.

How Parenting Changes

Part of launching our children successfully involves understanding how parenting changes over the years. As a father of four young children, I could barely look more than a year or two into the future. I was just trying to figure things out and survive. But having raised those children to adulthood, I can tell you with certainty there are different seasons of parenting. And if you do not understand those, you will have launch problems.

One set of terms for the different seasons might be labeled *cop*, *communicator*, *coach*, and *consultant*.[3] I call this the parenting success sequence. When your children are young, the most immediate goal is to see that they obey you. Though you certainly want to provide lots of affection and warmth, the main goal is securing obedience. During the ages of six to twelve, you're communicating more deeply as their ability to comprehend increases. As they mature even more, you start becoming less direct and move into a coaching phase. You are still an authority but they are the ones in the game. You can call time-out if you need to, but you cannot stop the game. This is an excellent time to give more freedom and even expect some failures. For example, we let them drive a car knowing they might receive a ticket or have a small fender-bender. But they are in the home to coach them on these issues.

Finally, a parent moves to consultant. Your influence is important but limited. Here your advice is infrequent and may or may not be heeded. With this understanding, we add a question to be answered. Not only should we ask, "How do I launch my teen into adulthood?" But we also ask, "How do I go about transitioning from coach to consultant?" Our time of direct influence will be over. We are not "parenting" anymore. Direct instruction, routines, and discipline have come to an end.

Another analogy uses the word-picture of walking with them. When they are young you are walking in front of them showing them the way. When they are teens, you are walking beside them and giving input. When they are adults, you are walking behind them giving encouragement and just a little coaching.[4]

No matter their age, we will always feel connected to the heart of our child. Their joys will be our joys. Their pains our pains. What no one tells you when you start this parenting adventure is that your heart will be permanently connected to your child. Proverbs makes it quite clear that the wisdom or foolishness of a child does affect his parents. Truly, you are about as happy as your unhappiest child.

Where We Are Going

Now that we understand how parenting can change over the years, let's look over the structure of this resource. In this first section, we will seek to establish some foundational biblical principles. We will discuss a theology of age. This understanding will affect how we will think about changes to our children's responsibility to both society and God as they mature. The next chapter suggests some objectives we want to have as we raise our young people.

In the second section of the booklet, we will apply those principles to three different launch scenarios. Chapter 4 will help us think about sending our children off to a residential college. In chapter 5, we will consider how to launch them when they still live at home. And in chapter 6, we will consider scriptural principles to keep in mind when their presence in the home is difficult.

Cultural Bias and Unique Situations

I freely admit that my applications are influenced by my cultural background. I believe in the nuclear family and I believe in children standing on their own. Other cultures may disagree with the biblical principles and my applications. For example, I was recently speaking with one young man, a graduating college senior, who is a second-generation Korean-American. He told me that he is perceived as a child and expected to obey his parents until the age of thirty or until he gets married. Another young man from a Brazilian background still lives at home at twenty-seven. I am told this is expected. As I will argue in the rest of the book, in many cases, I do not think this is wise. Nevertheless, I know that I am making inferences from Scripture. Others may come to different conclusions.

In addition, although I will cover a few exceptional circumstances in chapter 6, I know there is a spectrum of issues that this booklet does not address. Mental health problems, addiction, or besetting health issues can all manifest themselves in the later teen years. Each of these would call for wisdom that is beyond the scope of this work.

Conclusion
Being a parent is one of the most humbling and challenging privileges God will ever give you. To make the challenge even more complicated, the execution of that influence changes over time. Once we think we have parenting figured out, something new happens. We know there are no perfect parents. But there are faithful ones. And that is what we will talk about in the following chapters.

For Reflection and Application
1. Have you heard of the metaphor of sending out children like arrows? What do you think of the aircraft and aircraft carrier metaphor?
2. Have you thought about how parenting changes over the years? Have you heard of the cop, communicator, coach, and consultant analogy? What stage are you in now?
3. What is your current plan to launch your children from your home? What are some pitfalls you may face?

2
TOWARD A THEOLOGY OF AGE

And [Jesus'] mother said to him, "Son, why have you treated us so? Behold, your father and I have been searching for you in great distress." And he said to them, "Why were you looking for me? Did you not know that I must be in my Father's house?" (Luke 2:48-49)

If we are going to launch our children well, we want to be intentional. Often parents will intuitively follow some of the principles we will cover below. However, if these principles are not clear, we can often react or overcorrect.

In this short chapter, I want to offer a tentative theology of age. I know that what the Bible *describes* it does not *prescribe*. In other words, just because a story is in the Bible does not mean God intends us to imitate it. Nevertheless, I think we can find some scriptural help to think about the teen years and the young adult years.

Thinking Intentionally about the Teenage Years

When we examine the life of Jesus, we find only one picture of his childhood. It is as he is entering the teenage years.

LAUNCH

> Now his parents went to Jerusalem every year at the Feast of the Passover. And when he was twelve years old, they went up according to custom. And when the feast was ended, as they were returning, the boy Jesus stayed behind in Jerusalem. His parents did not know it, but supposing him to be in the group they went a day's journey, but then they began to search for him among their relatives and acquaintances, and when they did not find him, they returned to Jerusalem, searching for him.
>
> After three days they found him in the temple, sitting among the teachers, listening to them and asking them questions. And all who heard him were amazed at his understanding and his answers. And when his parents saw him, they were astonished. And his mother said to him, "Son, why have you treated us so? Behold, your father and I have been searching for you in great distress." And he said to them, "Why were you looking for me? Did you not know that I must be in my Father's house?" And they did not understand the saying that he spoke to them. And he went down with them and came to Nazareth and was submissive to them. And his mother treasured up all these things in her heart.
>
> And Jesus increased in wisdom and in stature and in favor with God and man. (Luke 2:41-52)

We can see several principles quite clearly from this inspired account.

Jesus displayed independence. It was his family's custom to go up to Jerusalem for the Passover. Jesus had been there before. But this time, at age twelve, he displayed independence. Jesus left his parents and sat among the teachers in the temple, listening and asking questions. He evidently did not inform his parents. And when Mary corrected him for not telling her and Joseph, Jesus did not apologize. Instead, he gently corrected them by asserting the need to be in his heavenly Father's house. Scripture seems to have deliberately recorded this first instance of Jesus, at twelve, displaying a new adult-like independence and relationship with his Father.

Jesus displayed dependence. However, this was not a clean break into adulthood. Scripture tells us that: "And he went down with them and came to Nazareth and was submissive to them" (Luke 2:51). In other words, Jesus was still under their care. He still had some maturing to do and was still under their direction. The next verse tells us, "And Jesus increased in wisdom and in stature and in favor with God and man" (Luke 2:52). This well-known verse is a description of Jesus *as a teenager.* He still needed to grow mentally, physically, spiritually, and socially.

An Adult-in-Training

What can we learn from this brief vignette of Jesus at twelve? Here we gain a picture of him entering a new stage of development. Jesus was not a child but neither was he a full-grown man.

In our own experience, we can see this change taking place in children all around us. Our son or daughter is becoming an adult. Their body is changing. Their understanding is growing. They often vacillate between childlike foolishness and adultlike responsibility. Even they can't understand their emotions at times. But something is rapidly changing.

This season of a young person's life is acknowledged with coming-of-age ceremonies in different religions and in different cultures. Even in our secular culture, we start using the term "teenager" to refer to someone who is not a child but is also not an adult. We are told the teenage years are a time to detach from parents, push against society's expectations, and become an independent person. It is a time when friends become more important than parents.

In our family, we consciously labelled these years the adult-in-training years. When our children turned twelve, we told them we would no longer treat them like a child. Their twelfth and thirteenth years were a milestone. They were not adults yet, but they had started the preparation period. We were consciously seeking to give them more independence and responsibility. We wanted to launch them well. As long as they were responsible, they would be given more and more freedom.

We will return to this adult-in-training concept in the next chapter.

Thinking Intentionally about Adulthood

If the previous scriptures helped us to start thinking rightly about the start of this period, then we must ask, "When does it end?"

The book of Numbers records a significant moment in the history of the nation of Israel and helps inform this answer. God had delivered his people from bondage to the Egyptians. He had covenanted with them by giving his law and taking them to be his people. And now he had sent them to scout out the land that he had promised to them.

Chapter 14 records an assembly of all the men. In that gathering, out of unbelief, the men rebelled against God's command. They refused to take the land. God in turn punished their unbelief. His decree was that they would wander in the desert for forty years until that unbelieving generation had died off. What is important for our question is this fact: men who were twenty years old at that assembly were held accountable for the decision and died in the desert. *Nineteen-year-olds were not* (Num. 32:11). In other words, the nineteen-year-olds were not seen as full adults, responsible for the decision to rebel. Forty years later, at age fifty-nine, these men entered the Promised Land. We can see other places in Scripture where twenty years old marks a demarcation of military service or inclusion in the census.[5]

What this implies is that around the age of twelve or thirteen marks the beginning of the transition to adulthood. And around the age of twenty marks an ending of it. We see similar markers in our culture. For example, in the United States, voting, military service, and drinking alcohol are all privileges clustered around the age of eighteen.

Emerging Adult

Yet we also know that twenty-year-olds are very young! There is still much more maturing to do. A quick glance at the biblical record reveals that priests did not start their service until thirty. And Jesus did not begin his earthly ministry until he was thirty.[6] Again, we do not want to draw hard and fast lines, but Scripture seems to be on to something we know from life: Twenty to thirty is a distinct time of development. *Emerging adult* or *young adult* would be a fitting label for this time. By using this term, both parents and child recognize the young person's status as an adult but also their need for counsel. It suggests that these years are a season of launching into the world and a time to humbly seek out counsel. To harken back to our airplane analogy, these years are both the runway and the early part of the flight.

Implications

This understanding of age is inferred, not commanded, from the biblical record. However, it does seem to provide wisdom and guidance for parents. It helps us know when training to become an adult starts. And it helps us think about when an age of dependence is over. Just as a healthy baby has nine months to get ready before he or she is propelled into this world, so a healthy individual knows that there is a preparatory period for adulthood that also comes to an end.

We Are Finished
Understanding this timing of age is important to two different parties.

First, it is important to the child. He or she is not merely coasting through the teenage years. The world is waiting. They are on the deck of the aircraft carrier. The launch is not here, but it is coming. Having a certain end time gives hope to the strong-willed teen that his submission to his parent is only for a limited time. It also gives an ending time for the timid teen who does not want to launch into the world.

Second, it is important to us, the parents. We need to know when we are done. No doubt the infant in the womb enjoys the comfort and warmth and security. But after nine months, the time is up. Both mom and baby are ready for birth. Similarly, this marker around the age of twenty helps us realize the time of preparation is finished. As parents, we may continue to encourage and counsel. We may provide some financial support. However, we are doing so not to our dependent child, but to our adult offspring.

As a parent, you may not want to be done. You may have regrets and want to keep helping them. Or you may be a single parent and feel the need to make up for what they did not have. But we need to realize that chapter of our life is over. Our child *is* an adult. They must learn to act like it.

This understanding can help prevent what has been newly labeled *adultolescence*. Adultolescence describes a person who is biologically an adult (presumable over twenty) but acts like an adolescent. He or she is unwilling to enter societal adulthood, assuming full adult responsibilities.[7]

Conclusion

God's plan is for all of us to mature. Infants grow for nine months and then are launched into the world. Something similar happens with our teenagers. Starting around age twelve and ending in the early twenties, there is an intentional preparation phase. In their twenties, whether they like it or not and whether we like it or not, much of the preparation has come to an end. They stand before God accountable as an adult.

Now that we understand the process, let's think about our objectives in this process. What exactly are we aiming at? We will discuss that topic in our next chapter.

For Reflection and Application

1. How does thinking about Jesus as a teenager cast a vision for what we are aiming for as we disciple our children?
2. What do you think about the adult-in-training concept with the beginning and ending age?
3. If you explained the adult-in-training concept to your teenager, how do you think they would react? Have you tried it?
4. Why do you think that some adults struggle seeing their child as a maturing teenager? Or letting go into the adult years?

3
LAUNCH OBJECTIVES

*And Jesus grew in wisdom and in stature and
in favor with God and man. (Luke 2:52)*

It is always my goal to think clearly and intentionally about issues. So when my oldest was six, I remember asking myself, "Where am I aiming as a parent? What is the goal?" I came to the conclusion that biblically, God has not just given us a baby but an eternal soul to influence. We want to do all we can so that they love and follow Jesus Christ.

But there are other practical objectives that are not directly related to following Jesus. As a young father, I was influenced by a now long-lost article stating that a Jewish father wanted to train his son in three areas. If he had taught his child in these areas he had successfully prepared him for adulthood. Those targets? A father should aim that his son is skilled in the Word, with work, and with a wife. Those three areas—loving the Lord and his Word, being able to provide for themselves, and being a good spouse—

guided our thinking as my wife and I parented our two boys and our two girls. Let's unpack those objectives in more detail.

The Word

Scripture tells us that parents are to teach their children the Scriptures. Children come to us ignorant of God's Word and must be taught it. You can find these commands throughout Scripture, but especially in Deuteronomy 6:6-9, Psalm 78:5-8, and Ephesians 6:4.

As a dad, I felt that responsibility keenly. I wanted to make sure my children were taught and learned the Word of God in a way that seemed pleasant to them. You, too, should feel that responsibility. Some of that teaching can come from you and your spouse. At other times the church can and should help us. There are numerous activities your family can employ in this goal: family devotions, faithful attendance at Sunday School, memorizing verses, attendance at camps and conferences.

The goal in all of this is that our adult children would know and love the Word of God. Of course, this objective is not limited to biblical knowledge. It includes a converted heart. We were hoping our adult children would have surrendered their lives, repented of their sins, and trusted the Lord Jesus Christ for his atoning death on the cross.

Though we cannot control the outcome, nevertheless this is the North Star that we were aiming at and should guide our activities. J.C. Ryle stated our goal this way:

> You cannot make your children love the Bible, I allow. None but the Holy Ghost can give us a heart to delight in the Word. But you can make your children acquainted with the Bible; and be sure they cannot be acquainted with that blessed book too soon, or too well.[8]

LAUNCH OBJECTIVES

We want to be able to say to our children when they are twenty-five, "You heard the gospel clearly. You saw it lived out, with plenty of mistakes, but with grace and authenticity." For more help with this objective you can download *The Disciple-Making Parent* audiobook at our ministry website.[9]

Work

The second objective is summed up by the word *work*. By this we mean that a child is trained in a skill where he or she could support himself and contribute to society. Jesus was a carpenter. Paul was a tentmaker. They would not be dependent on others unless voluntarily for ministry's sake. Furthermore, they would expend their energy so as to be of help to others. As we work, God himself is active, providing for others through the tasks we do.

There are also many smaller objectives underneath this goal. We want our children to have the character to work hard. We will want them to work well under authority, with teammates, and leading others. They also need to know how to work smart. There is a duty to develop themselves to the best of their ability and as circumstances allow. They will increasingly know the way God has made them so that they can move toward a job that fits their unique bent. In addition, we want them to become increasingly aware of the way the economy works and the opportunities that are available.

They will need to have their mind and skills developed. This will often involve school after high school. It needs to be understood that this time is to equip them to provide for themselves and to bless others. It is not meant to be a time of self-indulgent self-discovery. If they choose to do that, they can do it with their own money. In one sense they have a whole lifetime to learn some of these work lessons, especially through the emerging adult years. And yet through our conversations and training, they can be helped to lay a good foundation.

Finally, it is worth making a few comments on how this applies to daughters. Although men are called to be the primary providers in their families,[10] we also should equip our daughters to provide for themselves. Some have objected to this responsibility to give vocational training. They would argue that a daughter will be helping her husband and raising children. Given how our culture denigrates motherhood, Christian parents must constantly emphasize the importance of this high calling.

However, a fuller reading of Scripture and mankind's nature leads me to conclude it honors the Lord to also train my daughters to help others in work. Why? First and most fundamentally, our daughters are made in God's image and also called to cultivate the world.[11] Second, the best helper to a husband is one whose mind is well trained. Third, we don't know if they will be married. They may be called to singleness and need to provide for themselves. And fourth, the nature of sin is such that there may be times they need to provide for themselves or help the family due to abandonment or disability. As a pastor, I have seen this latter situation more times than I wish.

A Wife

This brings us naturally to a third objective for a child. We continue with the word that begins with a *w* for alliteration's sake—wife. But this objective has the goal of helping a son or daughter prepare to lead in a family. It starts with parents demonstrating a healthy marriage that the children observe as they grow up. It continues with encouraging healthy dating relationships and respect for the opposite sex. It means we teach them the relational skills needed such as self-control, responsibility, listening, working through conflict, and asking forgiveness. We may even give some pointed encouragement about how to choose a spouse wisely. We want to teach them about the blessings and hard work of marriage. We also model and teach the basics of being a good parent and cast a vision for them doing the same.

This objective of relational wisdom is found not only in a commitment to a spouse but in a commitment to a local church. The local church is the bride of Christ. She is important to him. Even with all her flaws, she should be important to us. Church is a place we find teaching, accountability, friendships, community, wisdom, and the support we need to live the Christian life. We want to cast a vision for conscious commitment to her in the life of our children.

These three objectives—Word, work, wife—helped categorize a number of character qualities and skills that make for responsible and successful adults. But of course, these are not exhaustive. And there were three more that were particularly important to us.

Confidence

One of those other objectives became clear after Sharon and I sat down with her parents. We asked them, "What goals did you have for your children as you raised them?" Among their answers to that question, one stood out—confidence. We reflected on that answer for a long time. We, too, wanted to raise children that were confident. We hoped they would launch out into the world, meeting new people, and handling new situations. They would have the strength to overcome the normal setbacks of life and persevere. We did not want them to be prideful. But we did want them to be confident in the way God had made them and his ability to bring them through the trials he would bring their way.

As a result, in the childhood and teen years, we were regularly encouraging them and exposing them to testing situations. We were not bubble-wrapping them and trying to protect them from any failure. This is the exact opposite of today's helicopter parent. We wanted to coach them through the normal trials of life. It meant we allowed them to fall down as toddlers or teens. For one child, it meant cliff jumping and working in the inner city. For another child it meant participating in speech tournaments and not always winning. Adults need courage and confidence to face life. As our children overcame these obstacles, they grew in confidence. We want to raise our children to have grit.

Warm Connections with Us and Their Siblings

In addition, we hoped to continue a warm heart connection with us. We wanted to raise them to be independent *and* interdependent. While we rightly want to launch them into the world as independent, Scripture makes clear our hearts are always connected.[12] That connection can be frayed or it can be strong. A dependent, young-child relationship in which I am an authority grows into one in which I am a mentor and friend.

I have heard of too many children in their twenties who have turned their backs on their parents. Sometimes it seems much of the fault lies with the children. At other times, it seems the parents are the problem. I cannot control what my children do. But I can be aware of that potential problem. At the very least, I can aim to have a warm adult relationship as a goal and do all that is in my power to see that happen.

This means that during their childhood and teen years, I am parenting with both authority and affection. It means we are trying to make our home a place of joy and fun. We are reflecting the Trinity when we have honor and obedience as well as love and joy. It means building warm memories of fishing, basketball, donut dates, or "wrestle-time." All those are working to a warm-hearted adult relationship.

A related goal is that they will have warm relationships with their siblings. Perhaps this was easier in our family because our four children were each born two years apart. They were close enough in age to play with each other. Certainly, we had plenty of occasions for the normal squabbles. Instead of letting those go, we worked hard on having them ask forgiveness and make restitution.[13] It also meant that we tried to invest part of our small income into trips that built family identity and unity. If your children have a greater age gap, building warm relationships may be more difficult. Nevertheless, the vision of family unity and harmony is a good one.

Financial Independence

One final objective was also clearly understood—financial independence. Although I have already mentioned it in the Work section, it bears repeating here. We wanted to be clear that being launched into adulthood meant providing for yourself. Paul said that if a believer did not work, he was not to eat (2 Thess. 3:10). God has built a natural cause and effect into the world. As a result, surrounded by love and encouragement, it was clear that work was the next step after education. Whether they came back home to live for a short time or immediately moved into an apartment, the goal was always financial independence.

Conclusion

Parenting is a journey. Someone has said, "The days are long, but the years are short." Even as we enjoy each phase, it is helpful to know what an independent adult looks like and what we are aiming for. Having the goal to raise confident children equipped with the Word, for work, and for a spouse (wife), are good practical objectives to aim for. Now that we have laid a theological foundation, let's consider three different scenarios you might encounter.

For Reflection and Application

1. What do you think of the three-fold pattern of Word, work, wife? How does that help clarify your thinking?
2. Had you thought of wanting to raise confident adults? How does that affect your parenting of teens now?
3. What are you doing to seek a warm connection with your children?
4. Do your children understand how you are hoping to prepare them? Have you mentioned these objectives to them?
5. If you have a young adult, how do these objectives help clarify what successful "adulting" is?

PRACTICAL APPLICATIONS

4
LAUNCHING TO A RESIDENTIAL COLLEGE

At that time Jesus declared,
"I thank you, Father, Lord of heaven and earth,
that you have hidden these things from the wise and understanding
and revealed them to little children..." (Matt. 11:25)

Having thought about the principles, let's apply them to different scenarios. In this chapter we will think about a child that plans to go away to a residential university. Everyone does not need a college education. Some are gifted with their hands and need technical training more than a general college education. However, for our children, this seemed like the proper option.

On the one hand, this scenario presents several benefits. Leaving home is an obvious break with childhood. It is a transition moment. When he or she returns, a child realizes things have changed. It will never quite be home again. And that distance should be an obvious transition point for the parents as well. The tearful goodbyes as you drop them off at the dorm room for the first time helps establish the boundaries. "My baby is all grown up," she says. Not totally true, but definitely moving in the right direction.

Nevertheless, this is also a time when too many young people walk away from their Christian faith. Why? Scripture tells us that we are rightly influenced by pastors, parents, and friends. This is part of God's plan and the natural way of life. Yet, "going away to college" throws all three of those up in the air. Parents are often distant. Church commitment is questionable. And usually, the young person is making completely new friends. If he or she does not have discernment or is easily influenced, this is a recipe for disaster.

In addition, college is billed as a time to "find yourself," that is, to examine everything you have been taught. And who is helping a young person do that? A wise and godly person who has lived through the ups and downs of life? Not necessarily. Students can be influenced by professors with plenty of knowledge but little of God's wisdom; or they can be influenced by self-indulgent peers.

Let me balance that paragraph by recognizing and praising God for wise brothers and sisters who have persevered in gaining advanced education. I am thankful for those who faithfully minister in a college setting. In my undergraduate years I would have given anything to know that there were Christian professors at my secular university. Nevertheless, it is true that we give near universal, priest-like status to those who have earned a PhD. And they often see themselves as called to help those "small-minded" Christian students discover how their faith is bigoted and ignorant.

LAUNCHING TO A RESIDENTIAL COLLEGE

Advice to My Younger Self
As a young dad, I felt like I had a pretty good handle on my parenting philosophy and my discipleship philosophy. However, when it came to the pre-college years, my thinking was foggy. What principles should guide me? Looking back, this is what I would tell myself before sending my young adults off to college.

1. Do not promise unconditional financial help with college. Legally, I am done at eighteen. Any continued financial support is a privilege. It assumes my children continue their walk with the Lord and they continue developing marketable skills. That means that as long as they pursue these objectives I will try and support them financially. However, if they move in a different direction, my financial support can be stopped at any time. I want to make this abundantly clear to my children. My financial support is on a semester-by-semester basis. This is said with a heart of affection and love that wants their best. It is not meant to control them. I want to help support them during this time. It is merely meant to communicate that if they pursue different goals, they will do so with their own money.

2. Choose a college that has a strong on-campus fellowship and church. The best ways to find help against the temptations of college life and the deceitful philosophies is to stay connected with other believers, pastors, and college ministry leaders. There are better answers to every deceptive argument our children will hear. Other adults can help. You don't become a Christian by going to church but you do stay one by being faithful at a church. On-campus fellowships and churches near college can have dramatic spiritual impact during this crucial period of life. Parents, you can help make connections here even before your son or daughter arrives at campus.

In addition, they can provide friends that encourage them in godliness. Friends they choose during this time will have a profound impact on their lives. When looking at colleges, parents need to choose a school based on academic life *and* spiritual life. Unfortunately, I have watched too many young people with a good foundation veer off track without this fellowship.

3. Counter-intuitively, you might choose a larger school over a smaller school. Smaller schools tout the fact that their professors are able to interact more closely with their students. Often, in this day and age, that is exactly what you *don't* want! In some small colleges, the professors see their job as molding your child into their ("superior") image. In that case, the anonymity of a larger school might be better.

4. If possible, choose a school that is close to home or a relative. This allows you to stay in contact and children to connect occasionally for weekends and holidays.

Staying in Contact and Letting Go

But what about when my child is in college? The principle that should always guide us is that freedom is related to responsibility. College is another step of freedom. However, it comes with a test to see if there will be increased responsibility. And we want to communicate this to our child. Will they responsibly seek to deepen their walk with Christ and make their faith their own? Will they pursue courses that prepare them to contribute to their neighbor?

In all this, I am going to try and stay in contact without being overbearing. I am learning to ask good questions. To return to our launch metaphor, college is a time to launch the plane and stay in radio contact.

There are two pitfalls to avoid at this time. Some can assume their child is mature and does not need any more guidance. We believe if they have successfully launched from the carrier, then little discussion is needed. But even if they are young adults, they still need to be *wise* young adults. And a wise adult will continue to seek out advice.

This must be balanced with the newer pitfall to avoid—the helicopter parent who continues to hover over their children from afar. This plays out in numerous ways. I regularly hear of parents interacting with a professor concerning their child's grade in a class. If the child is not going to learn to work through difficulties in college, when will they?

Discussion Topics with the Child

What do we continue to talk about during these years? What are we going to talk about over "radio contact?" Although there certainly are many topics, I believe at least four need reemphasizing.

1. *The need for convincing.* Timothy's own spiritual experience puts words to the journey of second-generation Christians. In 2 Timothy 3:14, Paul encouraged Timothy to continue in what he learned and became convinced of. It seems that Timothy had learned the faith as a young child but he had to become convinced as he grew older.[14] Similarly, my own informal survey reveals that although many young people made a genuine profession of faith at an early age, college was often a time they made their faith their own. In other words, they were following because they were convinced. College can be a time of tremendous spiritual growth. Understanding this process can help them make sense of their own spiritual questions.

2. The need for good friends. Scripture says, *He who walks with the wise grows wise, but a companion of fools suffers harm* (Prov. 13:20). Paul even quoted a secular philosopher who observed that bad company corrupts good morals (1 Cor. 15:33). We will be influenced by the friends we choose to hang out with. Will our child be discerning in the friends they choose? The church or fellowship is the natural place to find those who will challenge and encourage them in their faith. What will their friend group reveal about their heart? And how will it shape their heart?

3. The need for good shepherds. We have a built-in need for guides. We will be influenced by someone. Will it be other godly influences, or will it be those who live apart from Christ? Our children should not expect to handle the distorted ideas on campus without help from others who have thought through these things. We are not only launching them to independence but to godly interdependence.

4. The need for wisdom and discernment. Discernment is the power of the mind to distinguish truth from falsehood. The problems of youth often come from a lack of discernment and lack of wisdom. Paul warned about false teachers deceiving the naïve (Rom. 16:18). We should encourage them to pray for and grow in discernment. College can be a place where half-truths are presented as whole truths. It is a place where deceitful ideas can poison their mind (Acts 14:2). Asking for advice and insight from others shows they are wise, even if not fully mature.

Conclusion

A residential college can be a great opportunity to grow spiritually or to drift away from the faith. An alert and watchful parent will choose that school carefully. With joyful affection, a parent can communicate the parameters that are acceptable in that decision.

For Reflection and Application

1. If your child is planning to go to a residential college, have you talked through your philosophy with them? Or are they going because "that's what everyone does next?"
2. What do you think about the author's advice to himself? Are there any principles you would change or add?
3. Did you attend a residential university? If so, how did that attendance help or hurt your faith? If positive, have you considered how much college has changed since that time?
4. Is your child "fully convinced" (see 2 Tim. 3:14)? If not, how will you communicate this need to them?

5
LAUNCHING WHILE STAYING AT HOME

But we urge you, brothers…
to aspire to live quietly, and to mind your own affairs,
and to work with your hands, as we instructed you,
so that you may walk properly before outsiders
and be dependent on no one. (1 Thess. 4:10-12)

In the last chapter, we thought about launching to a residential college. But that is not possible or even desirable for every child. There are a number of positive scenarios where a child would live in the home after graduating from high school. Perhaps a student desires to attend a trade school or community college while working. Or a child might move right into the work force while living in the home. No matter the scenario, he or she still needs to launch into adulthood. Thus, I have titled this chapter *Launching While Staying at Home*. I am thinking of a situation where the parent-child relationship is a positive one.

These principles would also apply to an older child who might come back to live with us for a short while. Perhaps they are a contrite prodigal who has returned home to get their feet on the ground. Or they might be a child who temporarily lives in the home for financial reasons. Two of our children came home to live for a year to help pay off some of their student loan debt. Another adult child lived at home for several three-month stints. These were all positive experiences for everyone. In the next chapter we will think about having children in the home who are presenting problems for the family. But for this chapter, let's think about a situation where a child has a good relationship with us.

Basic Principles
We start by reminding ourselves of the principles we have already established. God's intent is that we launch our child from dependence to independence. Twelve years old marks the beginning of that adult-in-training time. And somewhere around twenty, this transition period has come to an end. This does not mean our child stops growing and learning, but it does mean that they have reached an age of maturity. They bear the positive rewards of wise choices and negative consequences of poor choices.

If this is God's plan, then when we interfere, we are not helping our child but hurting them. One year our family bought a monarch butterfly kit. We watched the eggs hatch into caterpillars and then watched the caterpillars spin cocoons. Finally, butterflies emerged from those cocoons. All except one. As a family, we tried to help this butterfly by snipping the cocoon. But it never flew like the others. After some research, we realized a counterintuitive truth. By trying to help, we had actually doomed the creature. Butterflies need the struggle of emerging from the cocoon to invigorate their wings with blood. Without the struggle, they can never fully unfold their wings. They will never fly.

Similarly, our children need time of overcoming normal life obstacles. Without those, their maturing can be stunted. The challenges of finding a place to live, meeting new people, and balancing a budget are all ways that our children will develop confidence and grit. Just as pushing out of the cocoon stimulates life in the butterfly's wings, so overcoming these challenges builds maturity in our children.

Temptations

For a child who is continuing to live in the home, there may be some unique challenges. Perhaps it is because we slide into a new situation without calling attention to it. Our child thinks "My parents still have an open bedroom, so why wouldn't I just stay here?" When our children moved back in (at our invitation), I noticed an interesting phenomenon. We had a warm and loving relationship, but the setting encouraged two competing desires in them. On the one hand, they wanted to be independent, set their own hours, come and go as they please. On the other hand, they gladly let their mom shop for groceries, make meals, and wash their clothes. In other words, they wanted it both ways. Part of the reason it was so easy to fall into this was that we enjoyed having them home!

When an adult child is living in our home, we can easily revert to a pattern where it seems everyone is winning. But in the process, unless we are deliberate, we can be encouraging some future problems. They have not had to search for an apartment or struggle to figure out a budget. They are benefiting from our paying the mortgage, taxes, heat, electricity, water, insurance, and repairs.

Solutions

Instead, I would suggest that we as parents call attention to this new status and this new chapter in everyone's lives. Essentially, we would say something like this. "Mom and I have loved raising you. It has been both a challenge and a great joy. However, now according to the Bible, our responsibility is coming to an end. You are transitioning to adulthood. We want to help you out, but we need to come to some adult-to-adult agreements if you are going to live here while you go to school or work. These requirements reflect the advantages of us giving you room and board."

What might be those "requirements" we communicate or put into a Memo of Understanding? Following are a few you might consider.

1. Work. It is not wrong to communicate an expectation of work. This may be in the form of schoolwork or extra part-time work. But the point is that you are not going to subsidize them lying around the house or staying in their room playing video games all night. As image bearers, we are made to work, provide for our own needs, and bless others. Paul tied eating to working (2 Thess. 3:10). We are not helping our children by subsidizing irresponsibility. In particular, young men's self-respect seems to grow as they pay their own way.

2. Work in the home. In addition, it takes work to run a household. As children, they have benefited from our effort. However, part of being an adult is contributing to the normal workload that it takes to keep a household going. I remember one son remarking to me after he was out on his own, "Dad, daily life takes a lot of time! Grocery shopping, cleaning, laundry, and keeping the car maintained takes a lot of work." I just smiled.

Since everyone knows that the plan is to launch to independence, this time at home is a perfect chance to gain future skills. Call it an apprenticeship. Both young men and young women can learn a range of skills from cooking to automotive maintenance. Since their living expenses are being subsidized, they should also be willing to pitch in on a regular basis.

3. Pay room and board. I throw this in for consideration for our second scenario: when a child is working a full-time job while living in the home. There may be different scenarios when this happens. For us, it was when two of our children lived at home for a year. We charged them, not because we needed the money, but to train them in the practice of paying their way. Without this big expense in their budget, our child's temptation may be to waste money on extra items. There can be a false sense of luxury. Instead, we decided to collect room and board, save it, and then give much of it back to them when they left the house to apply toward a house or another large-ticket item.

4. Interact positively. Although we will talk about difficult situations in the next chapter, it is good to articulate this requirement here. Unless our child is living in an in-law apartment with a separate entrance and living space, they are still functionally part of the family. That means that they do not withdraw into selfish isolation. Instead, as appropriate, they are a cheerful presence in the house. If we ask them what time they are returning or make other house rules because of other children, they need to be willing to comply. This should be a non-negotiable. To not interact lovingly and work through normal disagreements is insulting. Again, we are training them to launch into normal life where adults are considerate of one another. This is what mature people do.

5. Go to a Bible-believing church of their choosing. Going to church has innumerable benefits for the young person no matter how strong or weak their faith. There are positive role models, encouragers, friends, and networking benefits. Studies show the positive life benefits of committing to a local church. We cannot control their commitment to Christ but we can decide that, if they are benefiting from our financial support, they will attend a time of public worship. And they will connect with other believers. Again, it is launching to independence and interdependence.

Opportunities

While the previous section has emphasized the agreement between a child and parent, we should not underestimate the benefits of a time like this. As mentioned before, we can use this time to train in life skills. We serve in our consultant role by talking about finances, car repairs, investments, or how to find jobs.

In addition, it is a wonderful time to learn from them. As we are transitioning to more of a peer-to-peer relationship, we can and should be influenced by them. Whether electronics, entertainment, or the latest trend, this can be a time to be instructed by them. It has been fun for our adult children to introduce my wife and me to new restaurants, new recipes, and new artists. An excellent way to keep communication channels open in this new relationship is to read something they are motivated to read or listen to a podcast that interests them. They are becoming an adult with their own contribution to life. When the relationship is strong, it is a joy to walk beside and learn from your adult children.

Conclusion

Having an adult child live with us presents challenges and opportunities alike. If God has called us to this for a season, we want to make sure we don't do this in a way that hampers our relationship and the maturing that God wants to do in them. But what about an adult child living at home when the relationship is stressed? We will think about that situation in our next chapter.

For Reflection and Application

1. How can living at home after eighteen possibly hinder a child from maturing?
2. What do you think of the author's suggestion for agreements? Which principle stuck out to you?
3. What do you think might be some challenges of having your child live at home? What might be some benefits?

6
STILL AT HOME WHEN THEY SHOULDN'T BE

"Then [the older brother] became angry and didn't want to go in. So his father came out and pleaded with him. But he replied to his father, 'Look, I have been slaving many years for you, and I have never disobeyed your orders, yet you never gave me a goat so that I could celebrate with my friends'." (Luke 15:28-29 CSB)

A mom approached me after a conference I had conducted.

"My oldest son is having a negative influence on our younger children. He is not walking with the Lord, but he is still living at home. What should we do?"

"How old is he?" I asked.

"Twenty-one," she responded.

"Then why is he still living at home?"

"He is starting his own business and we wanted to help him out."

With different variations, I have heard this question numerous times. Usually, the son or daughter is starting a nontraditional endeavor. Maybe they are attempting to start an online business. At other times, the child is taking a few courses online. And still others are working a few hours a week but have little desire to establish independence. Whether the older child is starting a business or attending college online or merely loafing, he or she wants the benefits of living in the home. And there has been an easy transition to this arrangement. After all, the parents are still providing for the younger children and there is an available bedroom in the house.

While this problem can be a temptation no matter which schooling option is chosen, it seems a special temptation for homeschoolers. For others, a traditional high school graduation provides a natural transition. Often a student's classmates are either attending further education or going off to work. Either way, there is positive peer pressure to make one's way in the world. However, homeschooling does not always provide those natural inducements. No matter the schooling choice, living at home too long can be a problematic issue for many.

Reasons for Special Temptations

Let's start by thinking about why staying at home might be a special temptation.

1. Feelings of failure by the parent. First, a parent may feel like a failure. We wanted our children to follow Christ as adults. But now we have come to the end of their teenage years and it is obvious our child is not walking with the Lord. So, either out of fear or guilt, this parent resists sending their child out into the world. Perhaps the child will not succeed, or they will fall under more ungodly influences. To use our launch metaphor, perhaps this child will fail to launch. Having them live at home with us gives us more time to influence and "help."

2. Feelings of guilt by the parent. Another motivation may be guilt. Single moms are especially susceptible here. Whether caused by choices they made or circumstances outside of their control, they know their children have not had an ideal upbringing. Moms can overcompensate for this deficiency by being lenient with their adult child. This may involve not pushing them out when necessary or rescuing them repeatedly.

3. Fear of failure by the child. A third reason might come from the child. Whether from fear of the unknown, laziness, or just inertia, staying at home seems the best option. It is safe and easy.

However, just as there is a time for a baby to leave the safe, protective womb, so there must be a transition point for the child. Though the baby may not want this new situation, it is ultimately better for him. Similarly, through the stresses of this different environment, the adult will begin the natural development of growth that God designed.

Convictions to Have

How do we approach this time? Everyone must be convinced of what we have talked about in chapter 2. There is a natural development from adult-in-training (or teenager) to young adult. The child in question has reached or is close to reaching the young adult phase. Our parenting needs to shift from providing and protecting. It is time for them to make their way in the world. They may not want the struggle. And we the parents may not want to watch the struggle. But it is good for them.

Part of maturing is learning that they are accountable to other authorities. God has set up the world so that you usually reap what you sow (Gal. 6:9). Sometimes mere words don't work (Prov. 29:19). They must learn consequences from others.

For example, if your child oversleeps for the job, their boss will fire them. If they don't pay their rent, they will be evicted. A good parent has sought to inculcate these lessons in the home. But whether or not the child has learned them from us, the time comes when he must learn them from others. There are other influences and authorities in the world to bring home the same lessons you may have been trying to teach them.

The child who is "starting his business" needs to get out and learn how that industry works. He needs to have the accountability of a bank or investors to discern whether his idea is truly a good one. The child who is "writing a book" needs real life experience to write from. She needs to write like every first writer does, finding scraps of time to pursue a passion, not subsidized by parents.

Without the accountability of the real world, we risk coddling our adult. We may be short circuiting what God wants to do through other authorities. Having the convictions that a twenty-year-old is a young adult will give us confidence to take hard but necessary steps.

Staying in Contact and Letting Go

What have I said to parents who asked me the question at the beginning of this chapter? In love, I would give this child an appropriate amount of time and tell him he needs to find an apartment and get out on his own. We give our child a deadline motivated by our care, explaining that it is ultimately good for him.

STILL AT HOME WHEN THEY SHOULDN'T BE

Proverbs 16:26 (NIV) tells us, "A worker's appetite works for him because his hunger urges him on." Starting out in a terrible apartment or driving a car on its last legs can motivate our child. It took the prodigal feeding pigs before he came to his senses (Luke 15:16).

However, unlike the prodigal who ran away, we can still communicate with our child. To return to our aircraft carrier analogy—we can still stay in radio contact. We can still express concern and empathy. We can coach with a few suggestions. We can even aid our child in the difficult transition by helping him look for an apartment, find a roommate, or work on a budget. This transition to the real world forces them to come to their senses or live with the consequences.

I once pastored a woman who came to Christ in middle age. She had two adult children and had never married. The daughter was grown and living responsibly. But the son, who was in his twenties, had a job but was dabbling in drugs. He was sleeping in the second bedroom of her apartment and not paying rent. After talking, she decided the best action was to give him notice and then move into a one-bedroom apartment. This single mom knew she would be tempted to subsidize her son if she could. But by living in a one-bedroom apartment, she was making it impossible for him to live with her except on the couch for a short time. This change had a wonderful effect. It caused him to come to his senses, get help for his drug habit, get vocational training, and eventually start a family.

Emergencies and Exceptions

Are there emergencies and exceptions to this idea? Yes, of course. Biblical wisdom is knowing which principle to apply at which moment. There will always be exceptions to the idea of an adult child not living in the home.

There may be an unplanned pregnancy by a prodigal daughter. There may be a job loss by a young couple. Or there may be a dramatic career change when the parents agree to help out their child and his or her family. As parents, we extend mercy in those moments. That's what family is for. We want our children to feel they can always go home. But that mercy is given and received as it is, temporary mercy for an exceptional situation.

In addition, there may be exceptional circumstances that require a longer launch time, even into the twenties. As I mentioned in the introduction, there may be mental health problems, addiction, or besetting health issues that can make it difficult to help a child into adulthood. My heart goes out to you. But God knows, sees, and cares. I would encourage you to seek outside wisdom as you attempt to navigate that turbulence.

Conclusion

Helping a reluctant adult leave home is hard on everyone. But whether butterfly or baby, the transition to independence is designed by God as part of the maturing process. We short-circuit that process when we provide what we should not. A wise son makes a glad father, but a foolish son is a sorrow to his mother (Prov. 10:1). As much as we may wish our young adult was wise and following the Lord, that may not be the case. They may be temporarily pursuing the way of foolishness. We do them no good by subsidizing this behavior. If our child is not seeking wisdom there will be consequences. Unfortunately, they must experience life for themselves.

For Reflection and Application

1. Are you in a situation where you are allowing a child to live at home even though it is disruptive? How did this chapter help?
2. Are you subsidizing their laziness or expensive habits in some other way? What negative results have you seen?
3. Why have you had difficulty launching them into the world? What reasons have caused you to delay this launch? Is there fear on your part or the child's?
4. What are some ways that you can start preparing them to live on their own?

FINAL THOUGHTS

7

FINAL THOUGHTS

When I was a child, I spoke like a child,
I thought like a child, I reasoned like a child.
When I became a man, I gave up childish ways.
(1 Cor. 13:11)

In the previous chapters I have sought to articulate some biblical principles and apply them to different scenarios. In this final chapter, let's step back and remind ourselves of the big picture. How do we launch our child well?

1. We want to parent with biblical wisdom. Wisdom is skillful living in God's world. It is knowing which principles to apply and at which time. In chapters 4, 5, and 6, I have sought to apply some biblical principles to general situations. They may nor may not apply to your situation. You need to decide for yourself.

For example, throughout I have emphasized having a young person be financially independent so as to mature. However, as I write this, I know of a friend who is letting his college graduate son live at home for a short while to save money. I know of another family who is letting their daughter do the same thing. In neither case is their maturity currently being stunted. You will need to decide how to take these principles and apply them to your situation.

2. We want to understand how our role changes over time. I have used the metaphors of cop, communicator, coach, and consultant to inform our thinking. This short book is aimed at ages where we are right at the end of our coaching career. We still have authority and may need to exercise it at times. But we are also starting to overlap with our consulting career. This resource is not about relating to them as independent adults.

A consultant knows that his livelihood depends on his relationship with his client. He may know more than the client, but he must present that understanding in a way that the client wants to hear. He knows how to ask good questions to understand his client's unique situation. In fact, some consultants get paid just to ask questions! Our role is changing and we will need to learn the skills that come with it.

3. We want to accept that our relationship will change. While the previous point focuses on relating to our child, this one focuses on *our* heart. Often, having poured much energy into our child, we don't want to let them go. But we must. They will make mistakes we could have foreseen. Some lessons they will need to learn the hard way. For others, we may insert ourselves at appropriate times.

Realizing our "baby" has grown up can be difficult for some parents. Though we have had many desires for them, we are gradually learning to cheer on their other (godly) desires. An emotionally healthy adult realizes he or she was given a child as a trust. God merely lent them to us for a season. There will be lots of surrender. We will also need to transition from what we want to what they want.

In the process, we must deal with our own feelings. I remember the sting I felt as I sold the baby furniture that had been put to good use with our four children. With a heavy heart, I realized that period of my life was over and never coming back. If we don't let go, we may find our relationship strained or broken. When parents cannot let go, often children think their only recourse is to cut off contact.

4. Treating them as adults, we communicate enough but not too much. As stated before, there are two errors parents can make during this time. One error is to think, "They are out of the house, they don't want to hear from me." The opposite error is to think, "We need to stay in touch so I can help them with life." While we are gradually letting go, they still need our advice.

This time of their life as an emerging adult is a time of turmoil and insecurity. Throughout their twenties our adult children are still facing many tough decisions. A young person is looking ahead and seeing their whole life ahead of them. Often, they do not know what vocational choices to make or they are tempted to make foolish choices.

Having watched them grow up, we know them best. And having lived for many years, we also know how the world works. My settled and stable walk with God will encourage them. My assurance that God will provide and God will direct can be a rock to them during this time. Our goal is to keep a warm relationship, appropriately passing on biblical and life wisdom.

5. Treating them as adults, we learn to communicate differently. If you are concerned about an adult friend, you don't immediately give direct advice. You may not even presume to understand the whole situation. You ask questions about the circumstances and their desires. You even ask what input they want from you. You realize your friend has to stand before the Lord with or without you.

Similarly, we are on the way to treating our child in the same way. They are growing into an adult with their own thoughts, desires, and bents. Our communication should reflect this depth. How do we do that?

We can become more skillful at asking questions.
Questions like:
1. What are some challenges you are facing these days?
2. What are you thinking of as solutions?
3. What led you to think this way?
4. This is what I heard you say. Is it correct?
5. Have you thought of other options?
6. Have you ever considered…?
7. What do you think I am not understanding about the situation?
8. How can I pray for you?

We can become more skillful at listening. Our children want to be heard and feel heard. They want to know that we are treating them, not as our little boy or girl, but as another adult with feelings and opinions. This respect may mean hearing critique we don't want to hear. Some of that critique may be true. Some may be youthful arrogance and wrong. But we want to listen with an open heart.

We can become more skillful at picking our battles. I will need to quickly learn to discern the importance of an issue. I may only speak about the one or two things I am most concerned about. On the other issues, I speak to the Lord, not them.

6. Treating them as adults, we encourage them in adult responsibilities and interactions. We do all that we can so that they are involved in a good church and receiving good input from others. We trust the Lord will bring other godly influences into their lives. A mature life is not independence only, but interdependence on God's people. It involves service to others. Maturity does not come just with age. It comes with accepting responsibility. And that means serving others in community. It means having a humble heart that seeks out wise mentors.

7. Treating them as adults, we differentiate between matters of right and wrong and preference. In a previous point, we have talked about picking our battles. Part of wise advice is realizing how important an issue is. There are of course, matters of right and wrong. There are also matters of preference.

Part of accepting this new adult relationship is processing their different convictions and choices our children will make. We will need to differentiate between what God's Word says and what are our preferences. On the former, I cannot bend. On the latter I need to remember that each one stands before the Lord himself (Rom. 14:12).

When I was a pastor, there were times that people would ask my advice and then make a different choice. These were not matters of sin but of wisdom. If, in my opinion, they chose foolishly, it gave me a chance to *pastor ahead.* My lead pastor has used this phrase to describe his strategy when someone is determined to follow foolishness or sin. Even if he has had to correct them, he wants to keep the lines of communication open. He communicates what he thinks they will face by describing sin's consequence. Then he encourages them to remember this conversation and his love for them. He wants them to feel free to come back to him later.

8. We carry the feelings they will never know about. We may have to deal with grief if they are a prodigal or choosing poorly. There may be worry over their future. They may cut off communication with us for a while because they are being foolish. Or they may withdraw because of our mistakes. All this emotion can cause us to talk to the Lord more. It should drive us to prayer.

All parents can look back and see mistakes. There are things we wish we did differently. Ever since Adam and Eve sinned, children have been raised by imperfect parents. If you are on this last page and feeling regretful, perhaps there are decisions for which you need to ask their forgiveness. But in this therapeutic age, parents can also take too much on themselves. Ultimately our children take our best efforts and stand before the Lord themselves. As individuals all of us are influenced by our parents, but not controlled by them. The actions they choose are ultimately their responsibility.

Enjoy Them!

And finally, we can enjoy them. We should not forget to delight in them! This is a person you helped create. You had the privilege of being one of the most influential people in their lives. Whether by presence or absence, our mother or father affects us deeply. We want to praise what we can, admire what we can, and encourage what we can. We imitate the Father when we express praise for our children and when we enjoy life with them.

FINAL THOUGHTS

Conclusion

Just like launching an aircraft, launching our children is serious business. For all involved, the engines are firing and the adrenaline is pumping. The anticipated moment is upon everyone. It is difficult to let the children we love launch from our house. But when we reflect more deeply, we would not want it any other way. This is what we have been working for. This is what they were made for—to soar on their own!

For Reflection and Application

1. Which one of these final principles stood out to you? How will you apply it?
2. How is your communication with your young adult? How could it grow? Do you ask enough questions?
3. How are you doing at differentiating between right and wrong and matters of preference? How are you doing in wisely communicating with them about those?

ENDNOTES

[1] See my material *Parenting with Confidence* at www.parentingwithconfidencestudy.com.

[2] See www.thedisciplemakingparent.com for more information and a free audiobook.

[3] My thanks to Dr. Rodney Navey from whom I first heard three of these labels.

[4] My thanks to Matt Schmucker from whom I first heard this analogy.

[5] See Exodus 30:14, Leviticus 27:3, Numbers 1:3, 1:18, 26:2.

[6] See Numbers 4:3, Luke 3:23.

[7] Clark, *Hurt 2.0: Inside the World of Today's Teenagers* (Grand Rapids, MI: Baker Academic, 2011), 12.

[8] J. C. Ryle, *The Duties of Christian Parents to Their Children* (Sand Springs OK: Grace and Truth Books, 2002), 8.

[9] Visit www.thedisciplemakingparent.com/freeaudiobook for the free copy of the audiobook.

[10] See Genesis 2:15, 3:17-18.

[11] See Genesis 1:28, Proverbs 31:10-31.

[12] Numerous verses speak to how wise children bless their parents and foolish ones bring grief. For example, see Proverbs 10:1, 15:20, 17:21, 17:25, 19:13, 23:24-25, 29:3. In addition, Proverbs 17:6 tells us that fathers are the glory of their children.

[13] Siblings can be trained to be kind and work through conflict. There are numerous articles on unity and forgiveness at our ministry website including www.thedisciplemakingparent.com/forced-to-be-kind.

[14] Paul recounted how Timothy had learned the faith and then become convinced. This two-fold process occurs in most second-generation Christians. For more information see chapter 2 of *The Disciple-Making Parent*.

Your children will either live forever with Jesus or apart from him.

Do you have a strategy for parenting in today's hostile culture?

The Disciple-Making Parent will give you confidence in your journey.

The Disciple-Making Parent
by Chap Bettis
ISBN: 978-0692671054

For your free audiobook of *The Disciple-Making Parent* or to receive regular parenting encouragement from the ministry simply send an email to audiobook@theapollosproject.com with *Parenting with Confidence* in the subject line.

Ashamed of your yelling?
Parenting with Patience will you overcome your anger!

For more information or to order in bulk visit
parentingwithpatiencestudy.com

Podcasts to help give you confidence on your journey as a parent.

A podcast that seeks to equip parents and churches to pass the gospel to their children.

A short-form podcast where I read my blogs in audio format for your convenience.

For more information visit
thedisciplemakingparent.com/podcast
Or search for The Disciple-Making Parent wherever you listen to podcasts.

www.ingramcontent.com/pod-product-compliance
Lightning Source LLC
Chambersburg PA
CBHW071410040426
42444CB00009B/2174